EASY Top OF THE CHARTS PLAYLIST
INSTRUMENTAL SOLOS

Arranged by Bill Galliford and Ethan Neuburg

Recordings produced by Dan Warner, Doug Emery and Lee Levin

mp3 CD Track

Contents

© 2017 Alfred Music
USA.

Alfred Cares. Contents printed on environmentally responsible paper.

7 YEARS

Track 2: Demo
Track 3: Play-Along

Words and Music by
LUKAS FORCHHAMMER, MORTEN RISTORP,
STEFAN FORREST, DAVID LABREL,
MORTEN PILEGAARD and CHRISTOPHER BROWN

With a slight swing ($\sqcap = \overset{3}{\overline{}}$)

Moderately ($\quarternote = 120$)

7 Years - 2 - 1

3

7 Years - 2 - 2

CAKE BY THE OCEAN

Words and Music by
JUSTIN TRANTER, ROBIN FREDRIKSSON,
MATTIAS LARSSON and JOE JONAS

Cake by the Ocean - 2 - 1

Cake by the Ocean - 2 - 2

Track 6: Demo
Track 7: Play-Along

HEATHENS

Words and Music by
TYLER JOSEPH

Heathens - 2 - 1

Track 8: Demo
Track 9: Play-Along

JUST LIKE FIRE

Words and Music by
OSCAR HOLTER, MAX MARTIN,
SHELLBACK and ALECIA MOORE

Moderate rock (♩ = 82)

RIDE

Track 10: Demo
Track 11: Play-Along

Words and Music by
TYLER JOSEPH

Track 12: Demo
Track 13: Play-Along

RISE

Words and Music by
KATY PERRY, MAX MARTIN,
ALI PAYAMI and SAVAN KOTECHA

Moderately (♩ = 100)

SETTING THE WORLD ON FIRE

Track 14: Demo
Track 15: Play-Along

Words and Music by
MATT JENKINS, JOSH OSBORNE
and ROSS COPPERMAN

Track 16: Demo
Track 17: Play-Along

ONE CALL AWAY

Words and Music by
MATTHEW PRIME, JUSTIN FRANKS,
CHARLIE PUTH, BREYAN ISAAC,
MAUREEN MCDONALD and SHY CARTER

One Call Away - 2 - 1

THY WILL

Track 18: Demo
Track 19: Play-Along

Words and Music by
HILLARY SCOTT, EMILY WEISBAND
and BERNIE HERMS

Thy Will - 2 - 1

WE DON'T TALK ANYMORE

Track 20: Demo
Track 21: Play-Along

Words and Music by
CHARLIE PUTH, SELENA GOMEZ
and JACOB KASHIR

Moderately (♩ = 100)

We Don't Talk Anymore - 2 - 1

Track 22: Demo
Track 23: Play-Along

YOU'LL BE BACK
(from the Broadway musical *Hamilton*)

Words and Music by
LIN-MANUEL MIRANDA

You'll Be Back - 2 - 1

*C♭ = B

You'll Be Back - 2 - 2

STARVING (UNTIL I TASTED YOU)

Track 24: Demo
Track 25: Play-Along

Words and Music by
ANASTASIA WHITEACRE, ROBERT McCURDY,
CHRISTOPHER PETROSINO and MICHAEL TREWARTHA

Moderately (♩ = 100)